ETIQUETTE ™
RULES!

DATING
ETIQUETTE
AND SEXUAL RESPECT

JENNIFER CULP

rosen publishing's
rosen
central®

NEW YORK

Published in 2017 by The Rosen Publishing Group, Inc.
29 East 21st Street, New York, NY 10010

First Edition

Library of Congress Cataloging-in-Publication Data

Names: Culp, Jennifer, 1985– author.
Title: Dating etiquette and sexual respect / Jennifer Culp.
Description: First Edition. | New York : Rosen Publishing, 2017. | Series:
  Etiquette rules! | Audience: Grades 5–8. | Includes bibliographical
  references and index.
Identifiers: LCCN 2016018361 | ISBN 9781499464948 (library bound) | ISBN
  9781499464924 (pbk.) | ISBN 9781499464931 (6-pack)
Subjects: LCSH: Dating (Social customs)—Juvenile literature. | Man-woman
  relationships—Juvenile literature. | Sex—Juvenile literature.
Classification: LCC HQ801 .C837 2017 | DDC 306.7—dc23
LC record available at https://lccn.loc.gov/2016018361

Manufactured in China

CONTENTS

INTRODUCTION   4

CHAPTER ONE
YES OR NO?   7

CHAPTER TWO
THE PRACTICAL STUFF   12

CHAPTER THREE
GETTING PHYSICAL   19

CHAPTER FOUR
BREAKUPS   25

CHAPTER FIVE
DATING AND FRIENDS   31

CHAPTER SIX
TOUGH STUFF   36

GLOSSARY   41
FOR MORE INFORMATION   42
FOR FURTHER READING   44
BIBLIOGRAPHY   46
INDEX   47

INTRODUCTION

The first rules of dating are simple:
1. Talk to your parents or guardians first. Dating without obtaining guardian-granted approval is a good way to get grounded.
2. Be nice. Always be kind to people you like as well as others you don't like. Be nice to people you go out with, be nice to people you turn down, and be nice to people who reject you. In short, be nice to everyone.

That's it! Dating is all about getting to know people. It's not a game, with points to be scored. There are no winners and losers because other people aren't objects like prizes. Like your friends, your crushes are just different people with their own histories, hopes, goals, and interests. If someone doesn't want to date you, that doesn't mean you aren't good enough. It just means that they aren't a good partner for you! Likewise, someone else's interest isn't an indicator of your worth. It's nice to be liked, but it doesn't make you better than anyone else.

One of the first steps in dating can also be the scariest. How do you ask someone out on a date? Follow two more basic rules.

1. Be respectful.

Is he dating someone else? Don't ask. Her parents don't allow her to date yet? Don't ask. But if you know your crush is single and there's no reason to believe your interest is unwanted, you're in good shape. They might say no—nobody owes you a date!—but they might say yes. You have to ask to get an answer.

Nobody is a mind reader. If you like someone and want to know if they feel the same way about you, you have to ask!

2. Make your intentions clear.

If you want a date, ask your crush for a date. Don't vaguely ask to hang out and hope your crush will somehow read your mind and get the real message. Say what you mean. "I like you. Would you like to go out with me?" is a pretty solid place to start from.

Asking someone out is really just the first step in the age-old practice of dating, but these basic rules apply to all kinds of situations. It's important to have respect for whomever you're dating, before, during, and even after you break up.

The intense emotions that accompany dating can make it feel complicated, but ultimately it's really simple: dating is about getting to know people, including yourself! Keep reading to learn more about the complexities that can pop up in any relationship and some ways to handle them that are healthy for you as well as anyone else involved.

CHAPTER ONE

YES OR NO?

The scary part of asking someone out is the looming possibility of rejection. It takes courage to tell someone you like them, and it hurts to hear "no" when you want to hear "yes." Rejection happens to everyone, though, and it's definitely not the end of the world. Getting turned down for a date doesn't mean you're undesirable or that there's anything wrong with you. It just means that your fantasies about this person don't quite match up with their reality,

Rejection isn't pleasant, but it happens to everyone. If someone doesn't want to go out with you, it doesn't mean that there's anything wrong with you, or with them!

and you wouldn't make good dating partners anyway. Remain respectful even if your crush turns you down. If he or she turns you down with unkind words, you definitely know that person wouldn't be a good dating partner for you: meanness is so unattractive.

HOW TO ANSWER

The first rule for responding to someone else's invitation to go out is the same as the first rule for asking someone out: be respectful.

HOW NOT TO BE A JERK

The method for avoiding being a jerk is really simple. Actually doing it can be hard, though, because it requires restraint. Here's the big secret: think about what you're about to say or do before you say or do it.

Is your joke likely to hurt someone else's feelings? Will sharing that particular picture embarrass one of your friends? Then don't do it! And that's it. Thinking about your actions is the easiest and best way to avoid being a jerk. At some time or another we all realize we've accidentally acted like a jerk to someone. Just apologize. They might not accept your apology and it might not solve the problem you have created, but it's one important step you can take toward not being a jerk.

Do you want to say yes? Say yes! Ask for any details you want to know about date plans. Feel free to say "yes" to the date itself but "no" to the activity if it's something that makes you uncomfortable. For example, if you're terrified of horror films, don't go along with a date to a scary movie just because you want to go out with the boy who asked. Tell him "yes," you do want to go out with him, but suggest another movie or activity. Only say yes when it feels comfortable. You are your own best advocate, so always pay attention to your gut feelings.

Do you want to say no? Say no! But do so kindly. Asking someone out takes a lot of courage, and someone who just asked you out has made him- or herself vulnerable to hurt feelings in hopes that you'll want to spend time with them. You never owe anyone a date for any reason, and you should never say yes to someone you don't want to date. You don't owe any explanations or rationalization either. Don't lie to try to spare someone's feelings, but take care to avoid being cruel. "No, thank you, but I'm not interested," is a perfectly adequate response. Remember: Respect is the rule, when turning down an invite and later when talking to your friends. Don't gossip about someone who asked you out behind his or her back.

Do you need some time before you answer? That's totally fine. "Thank you, I need some time to think about it," covers it. Do you need to ask your parents before you can say yes to a date? Be honest about it. Do you have to check and make sure you don't have plans with your friends that weekend? You don't have to have an answer ready immediately if someone asks you for a date, but you do owe them the courtesy of a yes or no answer eventually. Do not say "maybe" if what you're really trying to say is "no." And if you take some time to think about it and your answer turns out to be no? That's fine, but tell them: ghosting without giving a definite answer is mean.

TALKING ONLINE

We live in a digital world, and a huge amount of our communication takes place in non-physical spaces. Talking to people online is great! It broadens social horizons immensely and often proves educational. It can show you different sides of people, how they see the world through images and video, and how they express themselves with written language. It gives you means to express yourself in ways you might not be able to in real-world spaces.

So use social media to your heart's content! Talk it up over as many different apps as you want, but remember to:

- Be nice
- Be self-aware

Don't say anything you wouldn't want someone else to see in digital, capture—able form. Don't share information that's too personal. Don't share anything without thinking first.

HOW TO ASK...AND ANSWER

You can ask someone out on a date in all kinds of ways: a choreographed musical number, text, tweet, or snapchat. You can even ask by messenger pigeon or hot air balloon! Ask somebody out by whatever means you feel most comfortable, but take some time to think it over first. Any digital message you send can be made into a screen shot, saved, and shared forever. If the thought of your crush's friends reading your

Flowers are nice, but always remember: a gift is a gift, not a bargaining chip! Nobody is obligated to date you just because you did something nice for them.

message makes you feel embarrassed, maybe you should think about a different way to broach the question. When it comes to matters of romance, sometimes an old-fashioned in-person conversation is hard to beat.

As for how to answer? It's typically appropriate to respond by whatever medium the asker used to issue their invitation, but use common sense. Don't embarrass someone by turning them down publicly, if possible. Be nice!

CHAPTER TWO

THE PRACTICAL STUFF

Asking for a date seems like a big deal, but if your crush says yes, it's just the first in a long line of questions you'll ask and answer. Dating is a process of getting to know people, and talking is the primary means by which that's accomplished. Talking is sometimes intimidating! It can be nerve-wracking to work up the courage to say anything at all. It gets much easier with practice, however, and it helps to remember that, after all, it's just talking. Talking to a date is about communicating clearly and learning more about some-one else, not a game of trying to impress your date with the "right" answers you think they'll like.

HOW TO TALK ABOUT AWKWARD STUFF

First, you need to have a talk to plan the date. Where are you going to go? How will you get there? You need to ask to make sure you're both on the same page before the date begins. It can feel awkward to talk about money, but if the date requires expenditure it's important to make sure both parties under-stand who is going to pay. Sometimes it's easier to ask if you

Clear communication makes life easier. Be specific when making plans and discussing expectations and boundaries, and if you don't understand something, ask!

address the awkwardness of the topic up-front: "This feels weird to talk about, but when you asked me to go to the movies on Friday, are you planning to pay for both of us? I just want to know how much money I should bring."

Unless you stick to exclusively free activities, dating can get expensive. If you go out with a particular person more than once, it's not fair to expect the same person to pay every time. You can alternate payments, split the check, work out whatever system feels best for you, but you need to decide together. Talk about it!

Another important pre-date topic is parental rules. Does she have to be home by a certain time? Is he allowed to go

Group dates are fun and take off some of the pressure to carry conversation, especially when you're just getting to know your date.

bowling only on Tuesdays, in groups of at least fifteen people? You need to know before you go out. You don't want to get your date in trouble with their guardians, and you don't want to get in trouble for breaking a rule you didn't even know about. Ask if there are any special regulations your date needs to follow, and tell them about any rules pertinent to you.

"I have to be home by 9:00 on weeknights, but I can stay out 'til 11:00 on Friday. What about you?"

"I'm vegetarian. Do you have any dietary preferences that affect what you eat?"

Another potentially awkward topic that needs to be addressed early on is mutual expectations for the relationship. Are one or both of you casually dating multiple people? Are you expecting to exclusively date this person? It doesn't have to be a heavy conversation, but it's better to discuss it before feelings get hurt because of a misunderstanding.

A simple question to ask is, "Hey, are you seeing other people in addition to me?" or "I really like you, but I'm not ready for an exclusive relationship yet."

The best way to avoid miscommunication is to be open and honest. Think about what you want to say before you say it, be respectful and courteous, laugh about the awkwardness of the conversation, but say it. Don't make someone try to guess what you're thinking. Tell them! Likewise, never try to read anyone else's mind: always ask if something is not completely clear.

TONGUE-TIED

People are unique, and everyone has their own history of experiences and specific set of personal beliefs. When you're getting to know someone new, sometimes you might find that you disagree about some things. That's OK! It might be a big enough conflict of views to make you decide you don't want to date that person, and that's fine. It might be something silly, like whether you think gummy worms are tasty or disgusting. Regardless of the issue at hand, don't feel afraid to say, "I disagree."

On the other side of the scenario, refrain from picking at someone else over differences of opinion. A heated debate over the merits of gummi worms might be fun, but it's rude to hound someone about more sensitive, serious personal convictions.

The ability to apologize when you're wrong or you've hurt someone else is an important skill. Don't offer an insincere apology, though, or let anyone bully you into apologizing.

Sometimes a date might say something that feels offensive. Tell them. But don't fret if you don't react immediately. Many people freeze up when someone says something hurtful. That's totally normal! However, it doesn't mean that the offensive or hurtful comments were OK. If you don't discuss it immediately, bring it back up later when there is time to talk about it. People who care about you will want to know your boundaries so that they can treat you respectfully.

What do you do if you say something that hurts and offends your date? Apologize. It's not an argument, and it's not a matter of being "right": If someone else tells you that you made them uncomfortable, you should apologize for making them feel that way. Listen closely to other people and try to heed their words. Kindness doesn't cost anything, and respect lays a foundation for trust.

MYTHS AND FACTS

MYTH: The man should always ask the woman out on a date, never the other way around.

FACT: While this approach was not always a myth, the idea that a man should always ask the woman out on a date is outdated. These days, anyone can ask just about anyone else to go out.

MYTH: The man always pays for the date.

FACT: It's typical for the person who asked for the date to handle payment, but even that doesn't always apply. Not every dating couple is made up of a man and a woman, anyway. Any payment strategy that satisfies both parties is fine.

MYTH: You can only date one person at a time.

FACT: You can date more than one person at once. The key to non-exclusive dating is openness and honesty. If you're dating more than one person, each person you're dating needs to know that. If you expect an exclusive relationship when dating someone, that's fine too—just make sure to tell your dating partner.

CHAPTER THREE

GETTING PHYSICAL

hen it comes to physical affections, there are three big considerations to take into account: safety, comfort, and consent.

"YES!"

If you don't feel ready to engage in physical affection or certain types of physical contact, that's OK! If holding hands feels right but kissing seems like it's going too far, that's fine. You have the right to draw any boundaries you please, and you should set boundaries to ensure your comfort and pleasure. Don't say yes to any physical act unless you're 100 percent sure you really want to do it, and don't be afraid to say no if a date presses too far and makes you feel uncomfortable.

If you're the one initiating intimate action, always ask first. Always ask, even if it feels awkward at first.

"May I hold your hand?"

"Is it OK if I brush your hair out of your eyes?"

"Is it OK if I kiss you now?"

You need to hear an enthusiastic "yes" from your partner

Communication is sexy! Always ask before you touch. And if someone else makes the first move without asking? Smile and let them know you like to be asked first.

before initiating any new form of physical contact, and it must be reiterated, or said again, in new situations even if you've already done it before. Consent is key! Don't press beyond your comfort zone or your partner's comfort zone, and talk to each other throughout to make sure you're on the same page. You want your partner to feel pleasured, not pressured!

SEX

When it comes to increasing levels of physical intimacy, there's no substitute for planning. Sex is serious stuff. It can be amazing, and it can make you feel really great! But it's also dangerous, because it can result in things like sexually transmitted infections, unintended pregnancy, and—more commonly—seriously hurt feelings.

Sex puts you in a vulnerable position with another person, and you really need to know and trust your own wants before getting intimate with somebody else. Spend some time thinking about your boundaries and planning for any

Safe sex is non-negotiable. If anyone tries to pressure or shame you into having sex without a condom, they're telling you that they don't care about your health and safety.

eventual scenario: How will you ask your partner for the things you want? What will you say if your partner suggests something you don't want to try? Forethought and clear, open communication is the best way to ensure positive and enjoyable sexual experiences.

You've also got some practical work to do before you get down to the sexy stuff. If you're a girl planning to have sex with a guy or a guy planning to sleep with a girl, you've got to come up with and implement a plan for birth control. If you're anybody having sex with anyone, you need to have safe sex. Don't fail to plan and get caught off guard in the heat of the moment. Safe sex is the responsibility of both partners!

SAFE SEX ALWAYS

Maybe you're in love. Maybe it's your first time, and your partner's, too. Maybe you don't have any protection on hand but you really, really want to do it. It doesn't matter how passionate you both feel. If you can't have safe sex, always wait until you can. Safe sex is priority. If you care enough for someone to want to have sex with them, you should show them enough respect to have safe sex.

Furthermore, always respect yourself enough to insist on safe sex. Anyone who tries to pressure you into unsafe sex automatically disqualifies him- or herself as a sex partner. Their obvious lack of concern for your safety shows an unacceptable lack of respect for you.

If you're above the age of consent in your area, the choice to have sex is yours. However, you should talk to an adult before making the decision to have sex for the first time. If it's not a topic you feel comfortable discussing with your parents, you should seek out a trusted older friend or relative who can offer you good advice. A computer search engine, such as Google, can help you locate an accessible free health clinic or Planned Parenthood, and a fast anonymous phone call will let you know if the clinic can offer care without notifying your parents. Take care of your health!

Thinking, planning, and preparing might not seem as exciting as spontaneously making the decision to go for it, but it's the only way to respect and care for you and your partner.

THE DIFFERENCE BETWEEN COERCION AND REAL CONSENT

This can be a tricky concept, but it's really important to grasp: There is a huge difference between an enthusiastic "Yes!" spoken because you really want to do something and a "yes" offered for other reasons, such as feeling intimidated or worried that another person will laugh at you or stop liking you. "Yes" because you want to do whatever you're agreeing to is consent. "Yes" because you feel like you have to say yes is coercion.

If you feel pressured, intimidated, or frightened, you cannot give legitimate consent. If you are inebriated and out of sober control, you cannot give legitimate consent. Anyone who wants to extract a "yes" from you under any of these conditions is not acting in your best interest.

The experience of being coerced into doing something you didn't want to do can be extremely upsetting and confusing,

Pay attention to your feelings. If you feel uncomfortable or threatened in any way, don't ignore it! Don't let someone disregard your feelings or push you past your comfort zone.

and it can even make you feel guilty or complicit in your own violation. It is important to realize the difference between coercion and real consent both to avoid coercion and to understand what happened and heal if someone has used coercive tactics to hurt you. Pay close attention to yourself and your motivations. If your gut says "Yes!," that's consent. But if your mouth says "yes" while your gut is still saying, "I don't know....", you know someone is trying to coerce you into acting against your own instincts.

CHAPTER FOUR

BREAKUPS

H ere's the dangerous thing about dating. It can *really*, really hurt to get dumped, rejected, or dismissed. And it happens to everybody.

HEARTBREAK HAPPENS

When you like someone, you fantasize about that person, assembling a set of expectations. Large or small, you pin hopes to the vision you've developed around your crush, and when something happens to shatter that illusion in real life, it's horrible. The more you've invested in a relationship, the more it tends to hurt when it ends. If you've dated someone for a long time and become intimate, you don't lose only a vision of a future together when you break up, but also a friend, a set of inside jokes, a familiar routine, and a person to hold hands with. A breakup is a big loss comprised of a whole set of little losses, and it's completely natural to grieve.

A breakup can really devastate your sense of self-esteem. Breakups are always ultimately for the best—a breakup is a pretty huge indicator that you aren't a compatible match—but

The downside of dating: breakups. Getting dumped feels horrible!
On the other side of the scenario, breaking up with someone else
is nerve-wracking and guilt-inducing.

getting dumped can feel like being judged and found wanting. It's not true. Another person not wanting to date you anymore does not make you any less attractive, intelligent, or valuable. However, it can be really difficult to feel that fact when you've just been hurt.

It is absolutely normal to feel bad about a breakup, to feel hurt, sad, angry, regretful, jealous, even embarrassed. These are the most common emotions associated with breakups. You'd be foolish to assume you'll be the exception! But once again, it's tough to get your brain to accept the facts when your emotions are screaming something different. When you start dating someone you like, the butterflies in your stomach might assure you that you'll *never* break up...and then, when you do, it might feel like you are the only person in the entire world who has suffered such horrible pain. That's totally normal.

But it's *not* OK to behave badly because you feel bad. Here's where the "Be Nice" rule of dating applies ten-fold: You have to be respectful to the person you're dating, even when you're breaking up, if they dump you, or if they behaved cruelly to you. You might want to lash out at someone who hurt your feelings, to try to do or say something to make them feel bad too. Keep your dignity by keeping civil. You don't have to be friends with your ex, and you have every right to feel mad. Just take care to avoid channeling that madness into meanness!

HOW TO BREAK UP WITH SOMEONE

Other times, you might be the one who has to break up with another person. Maybe they did something hurtful to you. Maybe you've developed a crush on someone else. Maybe you just feel the relationship you're in has run its course, and

HEALTHY HEARTBREAK PROCESSING

Go ahead and indulge for a little bit if you need to: eat some comfort food and watch your favorite movie. Then put your pain to work. Channeling strong emotions into creative outlets such as music, visual art, dance, and theater is cleansing and empowering. Plus, it gives you something to do to keep your mind off of how awful you feel until you start feeling better.

A breakup is also a perfect time to try new activities. Gaining new experiences that you never shared with your ex helps to put distance between your current life and your old relationship. Making new memories with your friends is always a worthwhile way to spend time.

Important: be kind to yourself. Sometimes when you feel bad, you unexpectedly feel tempted to indulge in self-destructive behaviors that make you feel even worse. Make sure you eat regularly and get enough sleep. Never turn to substance abuse in an attempt to numb pain. Immediately speak to a parent or counselor if you feel tempted to harm yourself in any way.

Online, unfollow your ex on all forms of social media. You might feel curious about what they're up to, but it's not worth your peace of mind. Post-breakup social media stalking keeps your ex constantly at the forefront of your mind and delays your healing. Block, unfriend, and give yourself a break. Hurt feelings take time and space to mend.

it's time for it to end. It doesn't matter why you want to break up, but when you're ready to break up, you need to go ahead and do it. It's unkind to encourage someone else's romantic interest when you don't return their feelings.

As in everything else with dating, be nice. Think about how you would want the other person to speak to you if the situation were reversed. You don't have to apologize. You don't have to justify your decision or explain your reasons. But you do need to let the person know that you are finished with the relationship and that they are free to move on. However you handle the breakup—in person, over the phone, by text—do it respectfully. Think about what you want to say

Be kind when you break up with someone, but remember it's not your job to console them about the relationship's end. They should turn to their friends for comfort.

ahead of time. If you have any of their belongings in your possession or vice versa, make plans to return or retrieve them prior to the breakup.

It's tough to get broken up with. It's also tough to break up with someone in the right way. It can be nerve-wracking and scary to disappoint someone else, especially someone who likes you. It can also be scary to confront change. You owe it to both yourself and your dating partner to break up when you're ready to move on, however. Don't stay in a relationship because you feel sorry for someone. Don't stay in a relationship that is deteriorating in hope that it will magically get better. It's your responsibility to listen to your gut and honor your own feelings through your actions. Breaking up with someone else doesn't make you a bad person, but you need to confront it honestly. "Ghosting" or behaving badly in an attempt to get the other person to break up with you is manipulative and cruel.

When you break up with someone, they might feel angry with you. That's their right. Respect the person you're splitting with and give them space following the breakup. Don't try to force a friendship with your ex immediately; instead, give them time to heal and make new friendships. You might miss your ex at times even if you wanted the breakup—that's normal! But it's selfish to demand attention and validation from your ex once they become your ex. You once wanted to date this person, and the rules of dating still apply even after the relationship ends: be respectful, and be kind.

CHAPTER FIVE

DATING AND FRIENDS

Dating can be consuming. It's exciting, and it's easy to get caught up in a whirlwind of new romance and neglect your friends.

LOVE YOUR FRIENDS

When your friend starts dating someone else, it hurts to be pushed aside to make room for your friend's crush. The number one rule of dating applies to interacting with your friends while dating, too: *be nice*. Don't let your friends fall to the bottom of your priority list. It is extremely disrespectful to your friends to abandon them during the thrill of a new relationship and then expect them to support you when that relationship ends. Don't do it! And if you find that—in spite of your best intentions—you have been neglecting your friends, apologize and take steps to fix it.

If a friend disappears on you in the excitement of new love, take the initiative to let your friend know—nicely!—that their actions are hurting your feelings. Just like with dating, clear communication is vital to maintaining friendships. Honesty, consideration, and respect keep friendships alive.

Sometimes it's easy and sometimes it's tough, but be sure to prioritize your friends even when you're dating someone new or going through a breakup.

Prioritizing your friends doesn't mean that you have to tolerate bad behavior from them, though. Balancing dating with friendships can be tricky. Sometimes a new relationship can trigger jealousy between friends. Not even necessarily because both friends have a crush on the same person—a friend might feel envious merely because you're dating and they're single, or they feel left out of the excitement taking place in your dating life. Maybe they are going through a breakup of their own! A friend might act out toward you for any number of reasons, but none of them justify bad behavior. If a friend says cruel things, gossips about you, lies to you, tries to damage your other relationships, or tries to hurt you in any way, you don't have to put up with it to be a "good" friend. A true friend is respectful but honest. If a friend is hurting your feelings, let them know. And if you need to take some time away from a friend who has hurt you, that's fine, too. Immediate forgiveness is not realistic. Sometimes taking time apart from a friend who has hurt you is the best way to heal.

Likewise, if you have done something to hurt a friend, you can't force their forgiveness. Apologize and respect their wishes if they need space. A sincere apology and commitment to changing the hurtful behavior is the best thing to do when you realize that you're in the wrong.

FRIEND BREAKUPS

Friendship is important, but like romantic relationships, individual friendships sometimes don't last forever. That's OK! But like a romantic breakup, the end of a friendship is difficult and miserable. In some ways losing a friendship can be even more painful than splitting with a romantic partner, in part because there are fewer clearly defined boundaries with friendship than in dating. Rarely do you have an official "breakup" with a friend; and a lot of things might go unsaid.

Sometimes you don't get the closure you want when a friendship ends. It's difficult to process the end of a friendship emotionally in any case. Be conscious about what you're going through and give yourself permission to grieve. And remember, you can always appreciate someone for the friend they used to be even if you don't share the same relationship any more.

Breakups are also consuming. It's great to lean on your friends for support when you're hurting, but remember to pay attention to your friends' lives, too. Don't try to make your breakup and resulting pain the only topic of conversation. Your friends need your support for the stuff going on in their own lives, too, even when you're in the midst of your own overwhelming emotional crisis. Fortunately, thinking of your friends can help you get outside of your own head when you're feeling low.

CONFLICTS OF INTEREST

Every situation is different and yours might be an exception, but as a general rule it's usually best to put friends before romance.

What happens when two friends have a crush on the same person? What happens when two friends date and then break up? What happens if a friend starts dating another friend's ex? Conflicts involving dating and friends don't have hard and fast rules; the best resolution to each of these situations is unique depending on the people involved. Once again, the key is communication: you have to talk to your friends to work out the best way to handle your own particular set of circumstances. Once you've discussed the issue and understand how everyone feels, you can make thoughtful decisions about how to proceed.

TEN QUESTIONS TO ASK A RELATIONSHIP COUNSELOR

1. How can I tell if someone likes me?

2. What's the best way to respond if someone turns me down for a date?

3. How can I assure my friends that they're important to me when I'm excited about starting a new relationship?

4. How can I tell my date that I'm not ready to experiment with sex yet?

5. How can I tell my date that I do want to try something sexual?

6. What should I do if I feel that my partner is pressuring me into things I don't want to do?

7. How should I talk about future plans and goals with my relationship partner?

8. What are some healthy ways to process and express anger and sadness over a breakup?

9. What should I do if I notice that a friend is involved in an unhealthy dating situation?

10. How can I best support my friends through their experiences of new relationships and breakups?

TOUGH STUFF

Dating is all about people, and unfortunately people sometimes do bad things to each other. Sometimes people we like, trust, or even love do things to hurt us badly. If someone you trust does something terrible to you, it is important to realize that it is not your fault.

VIOLATIONS OF TRUST

If someone hurts you or tries to control you physically, that's abuse. Physical abuse is also a zero-tolerance offense. If someone deliberately physically hurts you, it doesn't matter if they apologize later. It doesn't matter if they were under the influence of alcohol or drugs. It is unacceptable and should never be tolerated. If someone you date makes you feel physically unsafe, you need to speak to a trusted adult or authority figure to get help.

Emotional abuse can occur in many different ways, such as if someone:

- Verbally criticizes or consistently makes you feel bad about yourself

Emotional or physical abuse can make you feel inferior and ashamed. If someone makes you feel bad about yourself, they're not a good partner for you.

- Tries to convince you that you not smart, beautiful, funny, or valuable
- Tries to interfere with your other friendships and isolate you so that they remain the only close relationship in your life
- Tries to make you doubt your own feelings and decisions in favor of their alternate version of events

Like all forms of abuse, this is zero-tolerance offense behavior. It doesn't matter if they apologize. It doesn't even matter if they genuinely feel sorry. Emotional abuse forfeits the right to a continued relationship. If you suspect someone is emotionally abusing you, immediately speak to a trusted adult.

Sexual abuse occurs in many forms, too, such as if someone:

- Touches you in an unwanted sexual manner
- Forces you to touch them sexually when you don't want to
- Sends you obscene comments or pictures or demands revealing pictures of you
- Intimidates or threatens you into doing something sexual that you don't want to do
- Does something sexual to you while you are unable to consent—if you are sleeping or impaired by alcohol or drugs
- Shares revealing photos of you without your consent
- Tries to convince you to have unsafe sex—even if you want to have safe sex with them

If someone sexually abuses you, it is not your fault. It doesn't matter what you were wearing, if you were breaking rules, if you're dating, if you didn't put up a fight, or if you had a consensual sexual relationship with that person before. When it comes to sexual abuse, the fault lies entirely with the person who perpetrated it.

Under no circumstances is sexual abuse acceptable. Sexual abuse is a zero-tolerance offense. Someone who has sexually abused you forfeits the right to enjoy a relationship with you. Whether or not they care about you, such a violation demonstrates an entirely intolerable lack of respect for you and your safety.

DATING AGAIN AFTER A BAD EXPERIENCE

Bad things happen. Sometimes *really* bad things happen. But life goes on. If you have been abused or suffered ill-treatment at the hands of a romantic partner or friend, it may be difficult to trust new people. Remember, you deserve all the time and space you need to heal from a bad experience. If you feel ready to start dating again, you don't necessarily have to discuss your history with a new partner first thing. You should explain any aspect of your past experience as it becomes relevant to your current situation, however. Respect, consideration, and plain old being nice are the most important priorities when you start dating someone new, and they especially apply to how you treat yourself. Don't push yourself past your comfort zone, and be patient with yourself.

It's hard to be vulnerable and open to new relationships after being hurt. Be patient with yourself! Healing happens in its own time.

If you think you have been sexually abused, you need to speak to a trusted adult to determine the best way to deal with your particular set of circumstances. Please see the For More Information section at the end of this resource to find a list of organizations you can contact to receive help and/or information.

If you are concerned that a friend may be involved in an abusive relationship, speak to an adult. Once again, look to the For More Information section of this resource to locate helpful resources.

UNINTENDED CONSEQUENCES

As previously discussed, unsafe sex is unacceptable. Don't gamble with your health and safety; Always insist on safe sex. Even then, there is a chance that sex might result in an unintended pregnancy or sexually transmitted infection. This is why planning is important when it comes to sex: if you've thought about what action you might take in any possible scenario, you will be better prepared to deal with it if the unexpected does occur.

If you suspect that you have contracted a sexually transmitted infection (STI) or you may be pregnant, you need to be examined by a medical professional. Depending on your age, you may be able to seek treatment at a free or low-cost health clinic without notifying your parents—call ahead to check. Regardless of whether you feel comfortable speaking to your parents about sexual problems, speak with a trustworthy adult. Your school counselor or an objective medical professional can always offer counsel in addition to anyone you personally trust to turn to for advice. Please see the For More Information section to locate helpful resources.

GLOSSARY

abuse Treating someone in a cruel or dehumanizing fashion. Abuse can be physical, emotional, or sexual, and it is never acceptable.

birth control Contraceptive measures to prevent unintended pregnancy, including condoms, hormonal birth control pills, and intrauterine devices, among others. Talk to a medical professional to help choose the right birth control method for you. Birth control is the responsibility of both parties in a sexual relationship.

boundaries Your own personal set of limits in which you feel comfortable and safe. A date should never ignore your boundaries.

breakup The end of a relationship.

choreograph To create a pattern of steps or movements, such as a dance.

coercion The use of force, intimidation, trickery, blackmail, or other tactics to convince someone else to agree to something that person doesn't truly want to do.

complicit Partially to blame.

consent Permission for something to happen or agreement to do something. Genuine, enthusiastic consent is required for positive sexual experiences.

crush A person who inspires giddy romantic feelings.

ex Someone you used to date in the past.

expenditure The action of spending money.

manipulative Characterized by any attempt to influence others' beliefs and behaviors through abusive, deceitful, or shaming tactics.

respect To recognize the value of another person and to treat that person with consideration.

romantic Related to or about love.

safe sex When people take appropriate precautions to protect themselves from unintended pregnancy and sexually transmitted infection, such as using a condom.

Sexually transmitted infection (STI) Safe sex is imperative, but some STIs can still be transmitted even with proper use of protection.

violation The act of failing to respect a person or object.

FOR MORE INFORMATION

Gay, Lesbian & Straight Education Network (GLSEN)
GLSEN New York City
110 William Street
New York, NY 10038
(212) 727-0135
Website: http://www.glsen.org/chapters/nyc
Through local chapters, GLSEN works to provide information,
     support, and resources for LGBTQ (lesbian, gay, bisexual,
     transgender, and queer [or questioning]) youth.

Loveisrespect
PO Box 161810
Austin, TX 78716
(866) 331-9474
Website: http://www.loveisrespect.org
Call, text, or chat online confidentially with trained peer advocates
     at Loveisrespect with any questions about relationships or sex.

Planned Parenthood of New York City, Inc.
26 Bleecker Street
New York, NY 10012
(212) 274-7200
Website: https://www.plannedparenthood.org/teens
Planned Parenthood is a health care and an educational organization
     that provides reproductive health care, sex education, and
     information to women, men, and young people worldwide.

Rape, Abuse & Incest National Network (RAINN)
1220 L Street NW
Suite 505
Washington, DC 20005
(202) 544-1034
Website: https://rainn.org

The Rape, Abuse & Incest National Network provides resources
and support for people who have suffered sexual assault.
If you need immediate aid, please call the National Sexual
Assault Hotline at (800) 656-HOPE (4673) to be anonymously
connected with a trained counselor in your area.

Seventeen: Dating Advice Aimed at Teen Girls
300 West 57th Street
35th Floor
New York, NY 10019
(800) 388-1749
Website: http://www.seventeen.com/love
Seventeen magazine provides helpful dating and sexual health
advice intended for teenage girls but helpful to teens of all sexes.

Supporting Our Youth
333 Sherbourne Street, 2nd Floor
Toronto, ON M5A 2S5
Canada
(416) 324-5077
Website: http://www.soytoronto.org/index.html
Supporting Our Youth is a Toronto-based community development
program designed to improve the lives of lesbian, gay, bisexual,
transsexual, and transgender youth in Canada.

WEBSITES

Because of the changing nature of internet links, Rosen Publishing has
developed an online list of websites related to the subject of this book.
This site is updated regularly. Please use this link to access the list:

http://www.rosenlinks.com/ER/date

FOR FURTHER READING

Byers, Ann. *Sexual Assault and Abuse.* New York, NY: Rosen Publishing, 2016.

Campbell, Gary, and Frank Hawkins. *Boy's Guide to Girls: 30 Pointers You Won't Get from Your Parents or Friends.* Sterling, VA: Big Book Press, LLC, 2012.

Eastham, Chad. *The Truth About Dating, Love, and Just Being Friends.* Nashville, TN: Thomas Nelson, 2011.

Fine, Debra. *Beyond Texting: The Fine Art of Face-to-Face Communication for Teenagers.* New York, NY: Canon Publishers, 2014.

Fonda, Jane. *Being a Teen: Everything Teen Girls & Boys Should Know About Relationships, Sex, Love, Health, Identity & More.* New York, NY: Random House, 2014.

Han, Jenny. *To All the Boys I've Loved Before.* New York, NY: Simon & Schuster Books for Young Readers, 2016.

Hemmen, Lucy. *The Teen Girl's Survival Guide: Ten Tips for Making Friends, Avoiding Drama, and Coping with Social Stress.* Oakland, CA: New Harbinger Publications, 2015.

Henderson, Elisabeth. *100 Questions You'd Never Ask Your Parents: Straight Answers to Teens' Questions About Sex, Sexuality, and Health.* New York, NY: Roaring Brook Press, 2013.

Kaplan, Arie. *Dating and Relationships: Navigating the Social Science (A Young Man's Guide to Contemporary Issues).* New York, NY: Rosen Publishing, 2012.

La Bella, Laura. *Dating Violence.* New York, NY: Rosen Publishing, 2016.

Lang, Amy. *Dating Smarts—What Every Teen Needs to Date, Relate or Wait.* Seattle, WA: CreateSpace Independent Publishing, 2016.

Levy, Barrie. *When Dating Becomes Dangerous: A Parent's Guide to Preventing Relationship Abuse.* Center City, MN: Hazelden, 2013.

Miles, Lisa. *How to Survive Dating.* New York, NY: Rosen Publishing, 2014.

Parker, S. M. *The Girl Who Fell.* New York, NY: Simon Pulse, 2016.

Payment, Simone. *Friendship, Dating, and Relationships (Teens; Being Gay, Lesbian, Bisexual, or Transgender).* New York, NY: Rosen Publishing, 2010.

Pons, Lele, and Melissa de la Cruz. *Surviving High School: A Novel.* New York, NY: Gallery Books, 2016.

Rowell, Rainbow. *Eleanor & Park.* New York, NY: St. Martin's Griffin, 2013.

Saltzman, Amy. *A Still Quiet Place for Teens: A Mindfulness Workbook to Ease Stress and Difficult Emotions*. Oakland, CA: New Harbinger Publications, 2016.

Skeen, Michelle, and Matthew McKay. *Communication Skills for Teens: How to Listen, Express, and Connect for Success.* Oakland, CA: New Harbinger Publications, 2016.

Testa, Rylan Jay, and Deborah Coolhart. *The Gender Quest Workbook: A Guide for Teens and Young Adults Exploring Gender Identity.* Oakland, CA: New Harbinger Publications, 2015.

BIBLIOGRAPHY

Culp, Jennifer. *I Have Been Sexually Abused. Now What? (Teen Life 411)*. New York, NY: Rosen Publishing, 2015.

Devoe, Noelle. "10 Things You Should Never, Ever Change for a Crush." Seventeen, March 24, 2016 (http://www.seventeen .com/love/dating-advice/a39058/things-you-should-never-ever -change-for-your-crush).

Fresh Air. "Teen Girls and Social Media: A Story of 'Secret Lives' And Misogyny." NPR, All Tech Considered, February 2016 (http://www.npr.org/sections/alltechconsidered /2016/02/29/467959873/teen-girls-and-social-media-a-story -of-secret-lives-and-misogyny).

Gordon, Emily V., and Ana Hinojosa. "How to Be in a Romantic Relationship." Rookie, October 20, 2015 (http://www .rookiemag.com/2015/10/how-to-be-in-a-romantic -relationship).

Masango, Lebohang. "The Dating Game." *Rookie*, September 13, 2013 (http://www.rookiemag.com/2013/09/the-dating-game).

Orenstein, Hannah. "21 Red Flags That Your Boyfriend Sucks." *Seventeen*, March 30, 2016 (http://www.seventeen.com/love /dating-advice/a39114/red-flags-that-your-boyfriend-sucks).

Planned Parenthood. "Consent and Rape." 2014 (https://www .plannedparenthood.org/teens/relationships/consent-and-rape).

Planned Parenthood. "Relationships 101." 2014 (https://www .plannedparenthood.org/teens/relationships).

INDEX

A

abuse
  physical abuse 36
  emotional abuse 36–37
  sexual abuse 38

B

birth control 22
boundaries 17, 19, 21
breakup 25, 27, 29–30, 32, 34

C

choreograph 10
coercion 23, 24
communication 15, 22, 31
consent 19–20, 23–24, 38
crush 4–5, 8, 10, 12, 25, 27,
    31–32, 34

D

date
  special regulations 15
  expectations 15, 25
  boundaries 17, 19, 21

E

ex 27, 30
expenditure 12

G

ghosting 9, 30
Google 23

M

manipulative 30

P

permission
  guardian-granted 4
physical affections
  physical contact 19–20
physical intimacy 21
safe sex 22, 38, 40
  safety, comfort, and consent 19
Planned Parenthood 23

R

respect 6, 8–9, 17, 23, 27, 29,
    30–31, 33, 38
romantic 29

S

STI Sexually transmitted
    infection 21, 40

V

violation 24, 38

ABOUT THE AUTHOR

Jennifer Culp is an author of nonfiction science, tech, pop culture, and health books for young adults.

PHOTO CREDITS